Pranks for the memories!

The Dandy and The Beano have been playing pranks on the world since their first issues – The Dandy in 1937 and The Beano in 1938.

Parents, teachers, pals and policemen were all targets for the comic pranksters. Great invention was used by characters like Roger the Dodger and Winker Watson to prank their way out of problematic situations. This collection of strips, selected from our archive, feature the art of the prank from many decades of these classic comics.

Original artwork of a Dennis the Menace prank from the fifties.

Dennis had a great imagination and the most unusual items had prank potential to him.

Mary, The Beano's merry mule pulls of a prank in 1938.

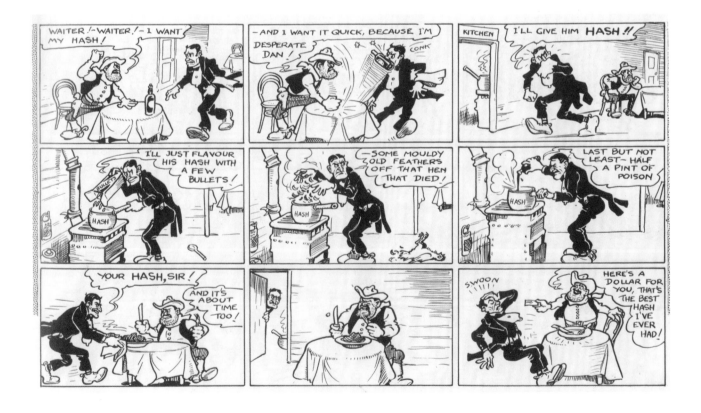

The Dandy was only three weeks old when the waiter pulls a prank on Desperate Dan.

Big Eggo the ostrich was the cover character of The Beano from 1938 until 1948. Most strips were stories without words but she was still able to pull off a funny prank.

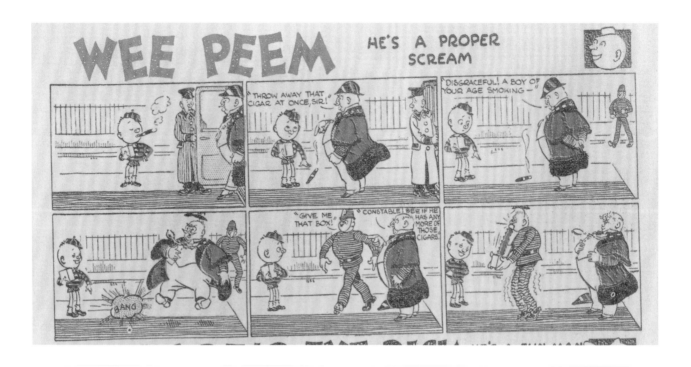

Wee Peem pranks the Mayor and a policeman in the very first issue of The Beano.

In the first issue of The Dandy, Smarty Granpa pranks his way to a winning throw.

No 176 APRIL 12TH 1941
EVERY FRIDAY.
2D

KORKY THE CAT

'HUMPTY-DUMPTY!' HEAR THE KIDS BAWL, 'COS HUMPTY-DUMPTY HAS MADE A TOUGH FALL. BUT KORKY IS BETTER THAN ALL THE KING'S MEN — FOR KORKY PUTS HUMPTY TOGETHER AGAIN!

I'LL PASTE THIS PAPER OVER THE COAL-HOLE AND IT WILL LOOK LIKE THE PAVEMENT!

Meet **MINNIE THE MINX** Inside — SUPER FUN FOR TWOPENCE!

THE **BEANO** 2D

EVERY THURSDAY   No. 596. DEC. 19th. 1953.

Biffo the **BEAR**

H'M—I'LL HAVE TO LOOK OUT FOR SNOWBALLS FROM BUSTER TODAY!

CAN'T SEE BUSTER ANYWHERE—AND I DON'T WANT TO, EITHER!

SOMETHING FOR YOU, BIFFO!

BUSTER!

LATER

BUSTER SEEMS TO HAVE GONE HOME! AH! THAT'S A FINE SNOWMAN!

HERE I AM AGAIN, BIFFO! TAKE THAT!

SPLOSH!

NOW TO GET ON WITH MY DELIVERIES FROM THE BAKERY.

BAKERY

HOI, BUSTER!

BALLOONS ALL SHAPES MADE TO ORDER

LATER STILL

AHA! IT'S MY TURN NOW!

BIFFO WITH A HUGE SNOWBALL! HAVE A MINCE PIE, BIFFO! MERCY!

HELP YOURSELF—BUT DON'T THROW THAT SNOWBALL AT ME!

MUNCH!

GUST OF WIND!

IT'S ONLY A BALLOON! BAH!

I'M FULL—AND YOU'RE FOOLED! TA-TA!

EMPTY

D. WATKINS

The ever hungry Three Bears set up crafty pranks to get themselves food. Mountains of the stuff. They were amongst the elite of comic prank merchants.

The pranks of schoolboy Winker Watson are part of Dandy legend. He called them 'wangles' and his nasty form teacher, Mr Creep, was usually on the receiving end.

By using some books and also his nut — Winker gets a motor out of a rut.

Next Tuesday — Creepy is dogged by bad luck — and Winker's dog has a lot to do with it!

DESPERATE DAN

THAT'S THE LAST OF THE TREACLE TOFFEE, AUNT AGGIE! I WISH YOU'D MAKE SOME MORE, BIGGER CHUNKS THIS TIME!

YOU'D BETTER GO AND BUY A BARREL OF TREACLE THEN!

HERE'S UNCLE DAN WITH THE TREACLE! I HOPE HE KICKS IT FAR ENOUGH FOR US TO GRAB IT!

SURE ENOUGH! I'VE GOT IT! HURRY UP AND SWOP IT FOR THE OTHER ONE, KATEY.

HO!!

IT'S ALL RIGHT, UNCLE DAN. HERE'S THE BARREL!

NOW TO MAKE SOME DELICIOUS TREACLE TOFFEE!

I'LL POUR IT INTO A BATH ON THE GAS STOVE!

THAT'S FUNNY TREACLE! —SNIFF— IT SMELLS MORE LIKE TAR!

IT CAN'T BE TAR! I BOUGHT IT AT THE GROCER'S MYSELF— IN GOES THE SUGAR!

IT SEEMS TO BE THICKENING ALL RIGHT!

BUT IT DOESN'T ONLY SMELL LIKE TAR—IT TASTES LIKE TAR TOO!

LATER

THAT'S IT READY NOW! I DON'T HAVE A TRAY BIG ENOUGH— I'LL HAVE TO POUR IT ON THE LOBBY FLOOR TILL IT SETS!

AT LAST

THERE! IT'S SET NOW! WELL, IF IT'S TAR, IT'S GOOD SWEET TAR THEN.

SURELY HE CAN'T BE EATING THAT STUFF!

MAYBE OUR TRICK WENT WRONG.

CRUNCH

SCRAPE

I MUST TRY A BIT AND SEE!

STOP THAT! THIS IS MY TREACLE TOFFEE!

NOW HOP IT!

OUCH! HE'S HIT ME WITH A CHUNK OF HIS HARD TOFFEE.

THAT'S KNOCKED ME FLAT ON TO THE NEWLY TARRED ROAD SURFACE!

WAIT THOUGH— THE ROAD TASTES LIKE TREACLE TOFFEE!

WHAT!

I MUST TRY SOME OF THIS! SURE ENOUGH—IT TASTES LIKE TREACLE TOFFEE!

M-M-M! IT IS TREACLE TOFFEE!

BOY, OH, BOY!

LATER

HO! WHERE'S THE TAR WE LAID DOWN HERE THIS MORNING?

WE'VE GOT TREACLE TOFFEE AFTER ALL! UNCLE DAN DOESN'T WANT ANY!

NO! THIS TAR TOFFEE IS MUCH TASTIER AND MORE CHEWY!

In early days pulling pranks was the work of naughty Beano boys but all that changed dramatically in 1953 when Minnie the Minx joined the team. Such a sweet little girl – such wild pranks.

ROGER the DODGER

A CORRESPONDENCE COURSE—HUH! THAT MUST BE LIKE BEING AT SCHOOL WHEN YOU'RE AT HOME! YOU WON'T CATCH ME BURNING THE MIDNIGHT OIL!

ENROL NOW
LEARN-A-LOT
CORRESPONDENCE COURSE
SEND FOR FREE DETAILS

JUST A MINUTE, THOUGH! THAT'S GIVEN ME AN IDEA FOR EARNING SOME EXTRA POCKET MONEY!

SOON—

I'LL PUT AN ADVERTISEMENT IN THE PAPER.

DAILY NEWS

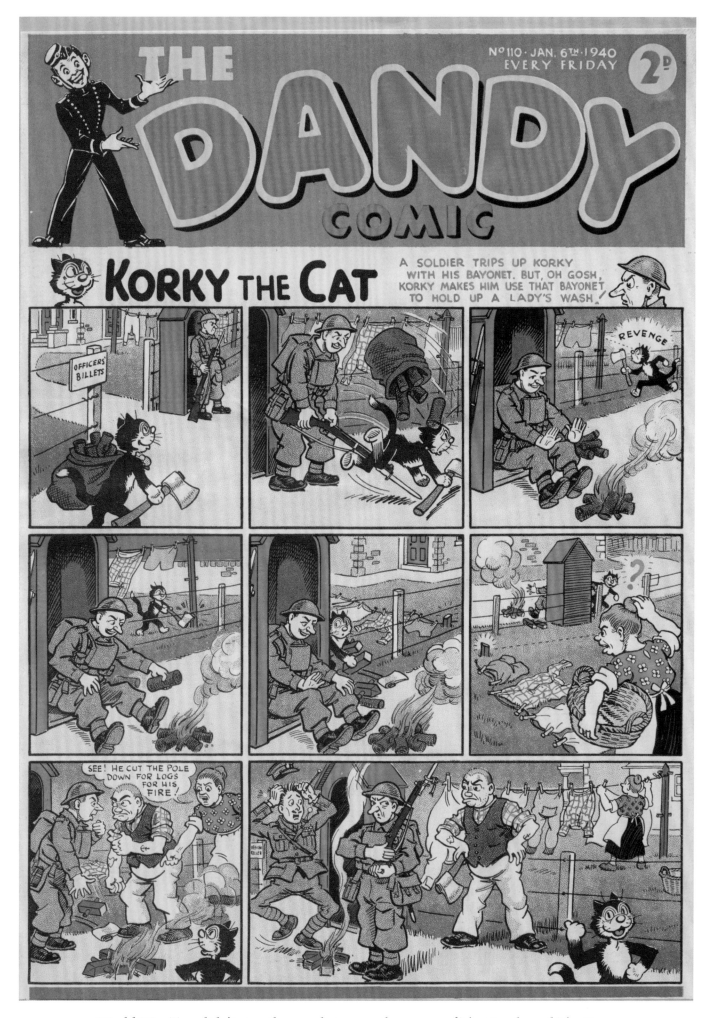

World War Two didn't stop the pranksters on the covers of The Dandy and The Beano.

THE BEANO COMIC

No 159 AUG. 9TH 1941
EVERY TUESDAY 2D

BIG EGGO

Dennis would often use a prank to try to con adults, usually his long suffering father, out of cash.

If Dennis had used as much brain power on school work as he did on pranks then he would have been top of the class. As this scam shows Dennis was amazingly inventive when it came to pranking teachers.

WELL! WELL! I'LL HAVE A GO AT THIS.

HOLIDAY SNAPSHOT COMPETITION
TAKE A FUNNY ACTION SNAP AND WIN A PRIZE

AND SO—
ALL SET TO HAVE YOUR PHOTOGRAPH TAKEN, DAD?
ALL SET, MINNIE.

BACK A BIT, DAD—BACK—BACK A BIT MORE—BACK—

— AND DAD BACKS INTO THE GOLDFISH POND!
YAROOH!
SNAP!
SPLASH
GOTTIT!

LATER—
THIS IS DAD'S DECK-CHAIR!
A TACK

HOLD IT! ANY MINUTE NOW!

THAT'S IT! ANOTHER ACTION SNAP!
SNAP!

C'MERE, YOU NASTY LITTLE BLOT!
WATCH THIS, FOLKS!

DAD SLIPS ON THE BANANA SKIN.
CLANG!
SNAP!....
GOODY! ANOTHER ONE!
SKID!
WHOOSH!

NEXT DAY
HEH! HEH! I'LL ENTER THESE THREE SNAPS OF DAD IN THE COMPETITION.

TWO DAYS LATER!
YOUR DAUGHTER HAS WON THIS DOG IN OUR HOLIDAY SNAP COMPETITION.
OH, BOY! A NICE TOUGH DOG FOR LITTLE ME.

FUNNY! THE DOG DOESN'T SEEM TO LIKE YOUR DAUGHTER.
HELP!
SNAP
— AND THE MAN'S RIGHT! THE DOG DOESN'T LIKE MINNIE AT ALL!

SEE!
HO! HO! WE'D BETTER CALL YOUR DOG 'CAMERA', MINNIE. HE LIKES TAKING SNAPS, TOO!

Grandpa was the oldest kid in The Beano. His greatest joy was to out prank the younger generation – namely the neighbourhood kids.

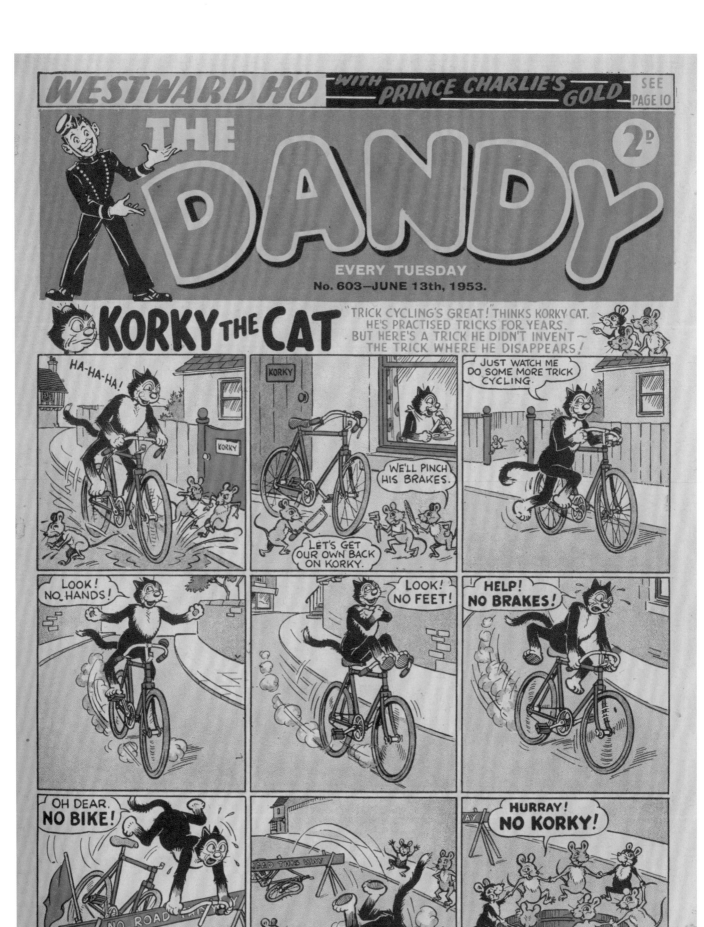

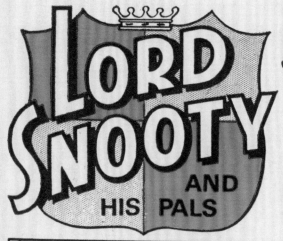

LORD SNOOTY
AND HIS PALS

I'M HAVING A BANQUET. I'D LIKE YOU ALL TO DRESS UP AS KNIGHTS AND STAGE A MOCK ATTACK ON THE CASTLE TO ENTERTAIN MY GUESTS.

THE GASWORKS GANG.

AFTER THAT THERE'LL BE A SPECIAL FEED FOR YOU!

AHA! WE MUST SEE ABOUT GETTING THAT FEED!

LET'S GET READY. SNITCH AND SNATCH, YOU CAN'T TAKE PART—YOU'RE TOO SMALL.

AW, SNOOTY!

BAH! NEXT THEY'LL TRY TO DO US OUT OF OUR SHARE OF THE FOOD.

HM! I REMEMBER THERE'S A PIT TO THE DUNGEONS UNDER HERE. GET ME A CARPET AND I'LL MAKE SURE WE GET OUR FEED!

SOON—

WE'LL ATTACK THE CASTLE FROM THESE WOODS.

HEH! HEH! THAT'S WHAT THEY THINK!

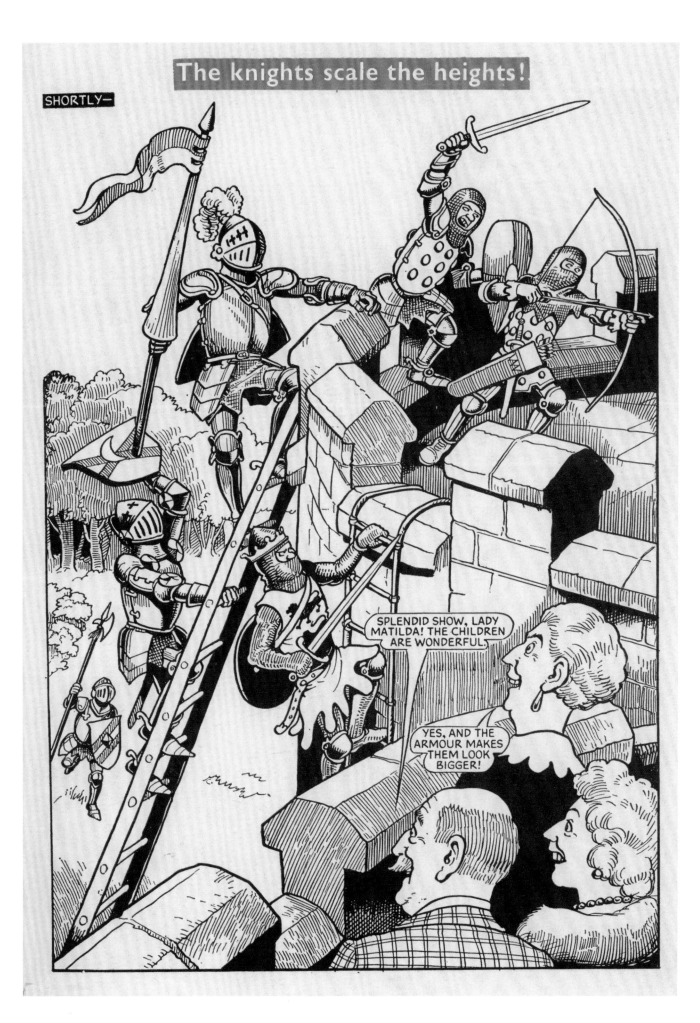

Snitch and Snatch make a catch!

BULLY BEEF & CHIPS

DENNIS *the* MENACE

I'M OFF TO THE FRUIT-PICKING TO EARN SOME MONEY.

YOU GO TOO, DENNIS. I'M FED UP OF YOU LOUNGING AROUND.

BUT I LIKE LOUNGING AROUND.

AT THE FRUIT-FARM— RIGHT, LADDIE YOU CAN CLEAR THAT ROW OF BERRY-BUSHES.

SLURP! IT'LL BE A PLEASURE, FARMER PRUNE!

SO— CHOMP! DON'T KNOW WHAT HE GAVE ME THE PAIL FOR — IT MUST BE FOR SITTING ON WHILE I EAT THE BERRIES! SLOO!

WELL THAT'S THE ROW CLEARED, FARMER, AND I MUST SAY THE FRUIT WAS DELICIOUS!

GRR! YOU'RE NOT SUPPOSED TO EAT THE FRUIT YOU GREEDY BOY!

HUH! PICKING FOR EATING'S OK, BUT PICKING ALONE'S TOO MUCH LIKE WORK!

THEN—

COO! — A HAIRY CATERPILLAR! WHAT A BEAUTY!

AH, WELL, THAT'S MY PAIL FILLED!

I'LL GIVE WALTER A SCARE!

PROUD

EEK! A HORRIBLE HAIRY CATERPILLAR!

SOB! HELP! MUMMY! SNIFFLE!

WELL, WELL, THERE'S A BIT OF LUCK!

PLOP!

THAT'S BETTER, LAD. HERE'S YOUR PAY!

COO! TWO SHILLINGS!

I'LL JUST HAVE ONE MORE JUICY BERRY BEFORE I GO!

LOOK OUT! THERE'S A WASP ON THAT BERRY!

YEEOW! SPLUTTER!

ZZZZZZ!

TEE-HEE! THINGS HAVE WORKED OUT VERY NICELY!

PLOP!

Printed and Published in Great Britain by D. C. THOMSON & Co., Ltd., 12 Fetter Lane, Fleet Street, London, E.C.4.

THE BEANO

EVERY THURSDAY   No. 500. FEB. 16th, 1952.   2ᴰ

THE BEANO

2D

EVERY THURSDAY   No. 640. OCT. 23rd, 1954.

Biffo the BEAR

SHAKE, PAL!

OUCH! YOU'RE KILLING ME!

I'M STRONG NOW. I'VE BEEN READING THIS BOOK.

MY POOR FINGERS!

HOW TO BE STRONG

I'VE GOT IT! I'LL FIX BUSTER!

LATER

SPORTS OUTFITTERS

FOLLOW ME, MEN!

THIS IS THE PLACE!

LATER STILL

HULLO, BUSTER! I'M JUST DOING SOME STRONG-MAN TRICKS—THEN I'M GOING TO DO SOME ON YOU!

GOSH, HE'S STRONG!

DON'T TOUCH ME, BIFFO— PLEASE, BIFFO!

TREMBLE

SHAKE

THEY'RE FIXED TO THE WALL, SHAKE, PAL!

FOOLED!

SHAKE

SHAKE

D. WATKINS

Multi pranks at the Bash Street School panto.

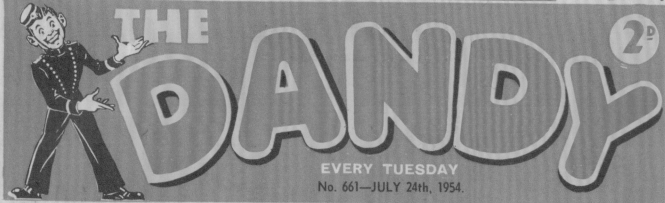

LOOK OUT FOR SHOCKS! **SHOCKER JOCK** IS COMING BACK!

THE DANDY

2d

EVERY TUESDAY

No. 661—JULY 24th, 1954.

KORKY THE CAT

A ROTTER'S SLICK WITH HIS DIRTY TRICK AND ENDS THE RACE AS THE WINNER. BUT KORKY CAT SOON SHOWS HIM THAT AT JAPING HE'S JUST A BEGINNER!

This story leads up to a crazy prank ending. Only Desperate Dan is tough enough to tame a haulage truck and play with it.

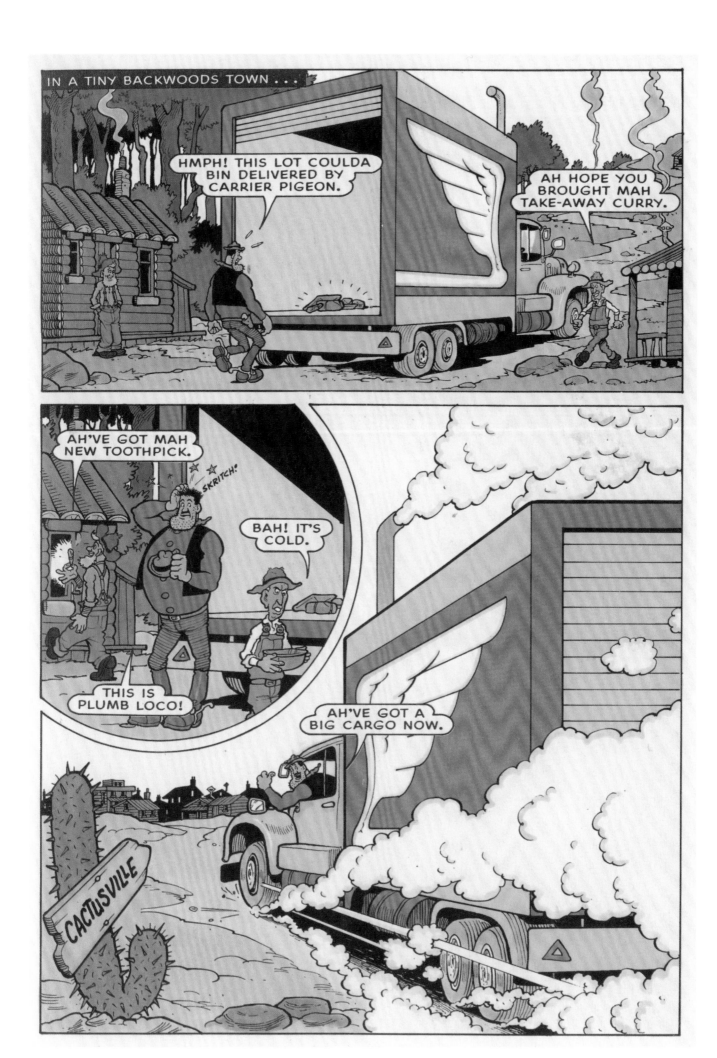

One more pace — and Roger's in space!

A painful stop to a parachute drop!

THE DANDY COMIC

No 17 · MARCH 26TH 1938
EVERY FRIDAY

2D

KORKY THE CAT

WHEN THE COPPER COPPED IT

Dandy Book 1965 and a prankster on the cover.

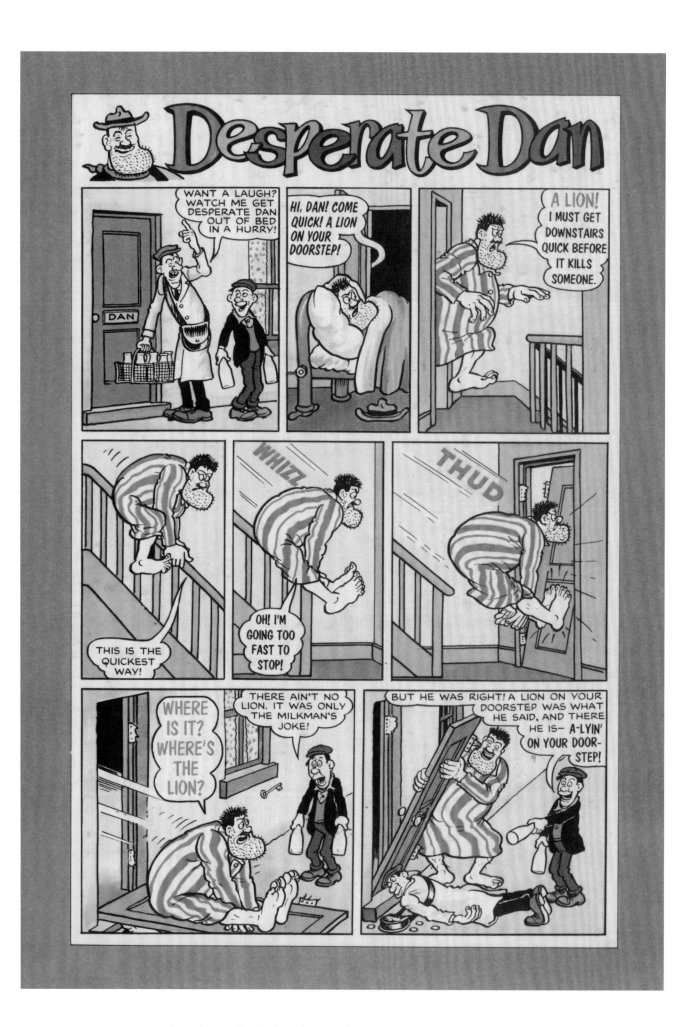

Dandy Book 1965 and a prankster on the back cover too.

Winker doffs his cap, and what do we find? — He has a cap and wig combined!

What's more, the class had dismissed in his absence!

Meanwhile Mr Sweeny had given Winker more than he bargained for, and now got rid of him at the back door.

Why was Winker picking up the clippings from his pals' heads?

Something queer about this, too. Was there a wangle afoot?

No, there didn't seem to be any wangle!

Form Three invaded the tuck-shop in force.

Winker's manners were shocking . . .

However, his mystery illness got him two free helpings!

Now for trouble.

CRUMBS! The barber's revenge had been to make Winker bald as a coot! So that was why the wangler had needed hair and glue—to make a wig!

MINNIE the MINX

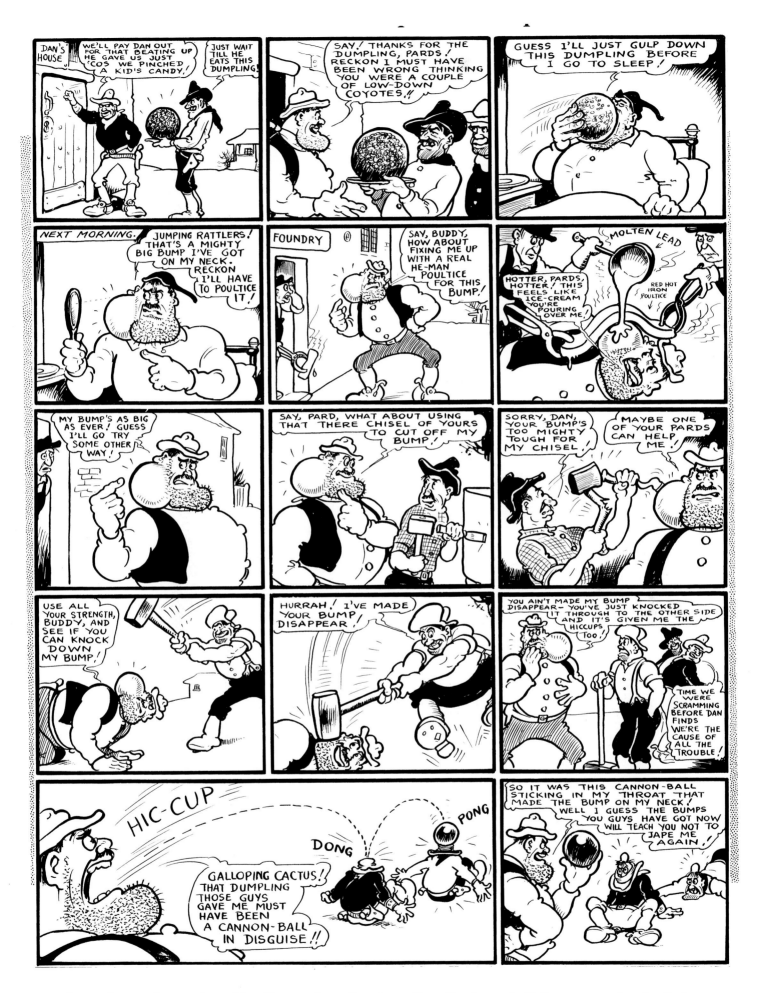

Who in their right mind would pull a prank on Desperate Dan. You know he'll flatten you when he finds out.

Dennis would use the most unlikely props to help him prank you – kitchen utensils were excellent.

The CHRISTMAS Beano

EVERY THURSDAY   No. 1327—December 23rd, 1967   3D

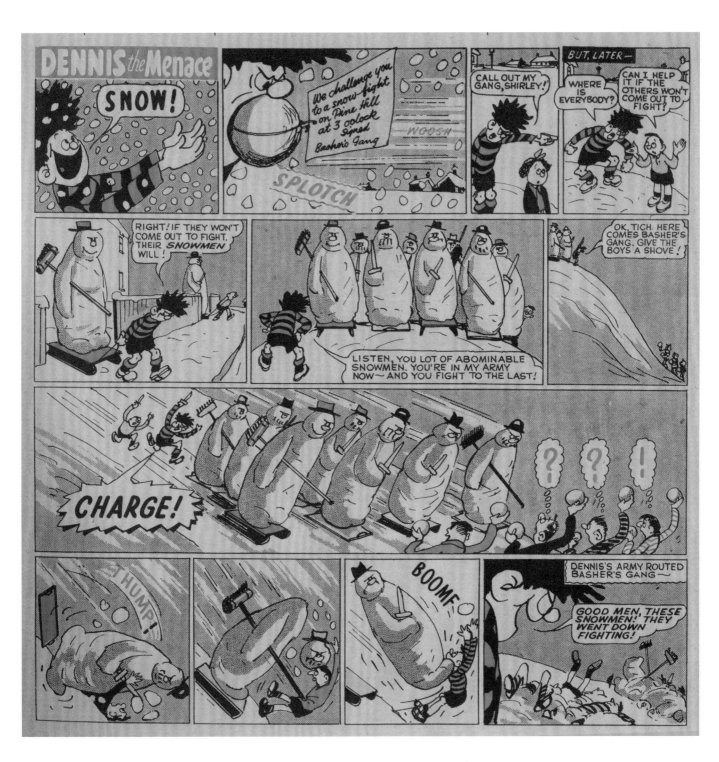

Dennis always rises to a challenge – especially if it's delivered by snowball. No men to fight Basher's gang with – no problem. Dennis will prank 'em.

Something Really Funny For Very Little Money!

THE **BEANO** 2ᴰ

EVERY THURSDAY   No. 604. FEB. 13th, 1954.

THE BASH STREET KIDS

THE BASH STREET KIDS

Pranks galore on this extra long school trip story. It first appeared nearly twenty years ago but the fun is just as fresh today.

The plot thickens!

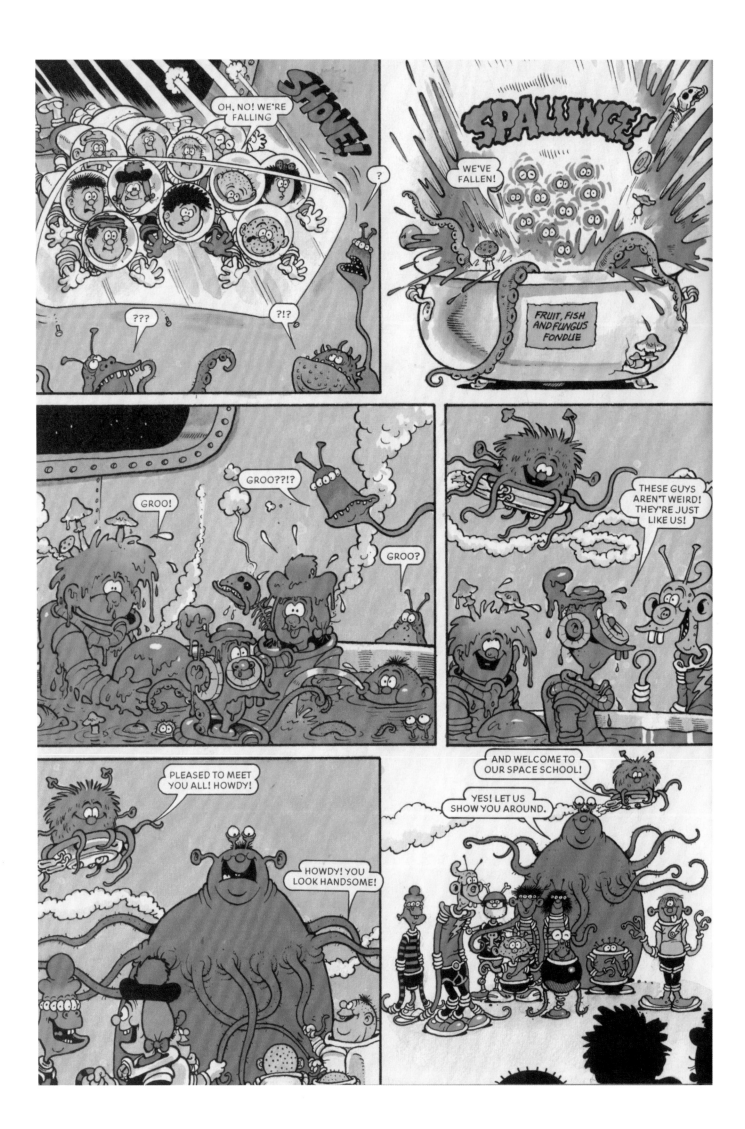

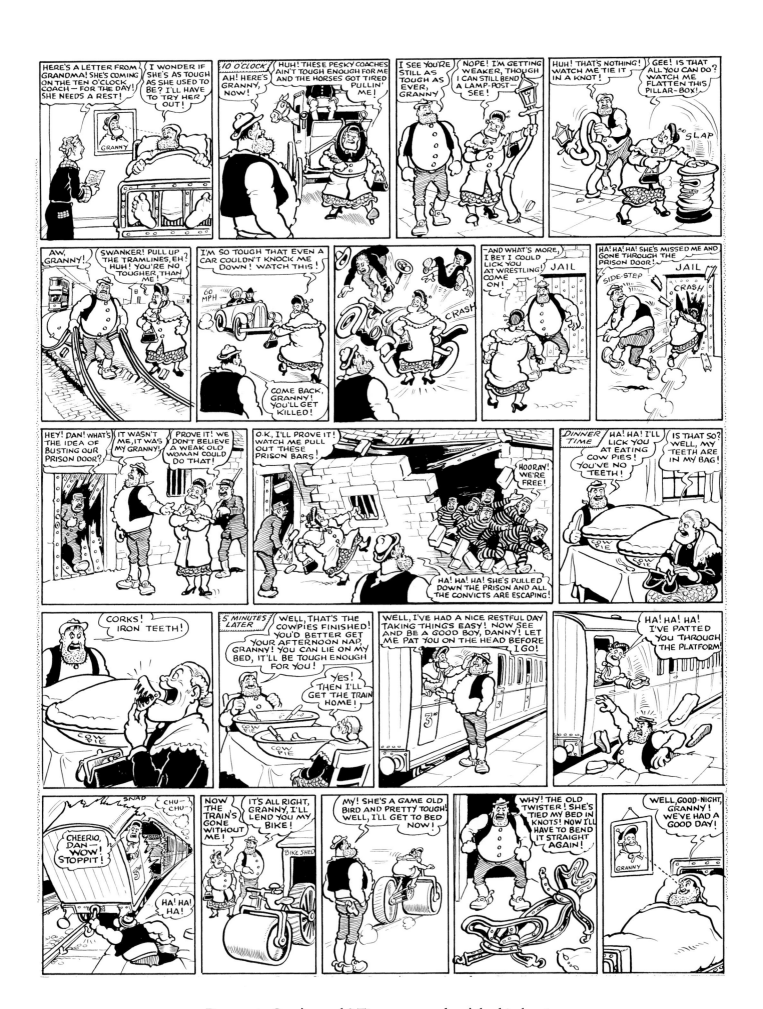

Desperate Gran's prank? Tie your grandson's bed in knots.

GOSH! Bunkerton Castle, where Lord Snooty and his pals stay, is the place for fun. There's always something happening there. The days nothing happens Aunt Mat sends for the doctor thinking the boys and girls must be feeling ill. Well, only the other day there was something extra funny going on. Snooty had been given a double helping of pocket money for being a good boy two days in succession. And he'd used it all buying a cheap load of rubber bricks. You should have seen these bricks bounce. What's more, being hit with them was like being clubbed by a feather. These rubber bricks certainly were full of tricks and no mistake!

Watch Lord Snooty's super toys make these bullies bouncing boys!

2. "Come on!" said Snooty, after he'd played about with the bricks for a while. "Let's show these bricks to our pals in town!" So off they all went with an armful of bouncy bricks. Their luck was out! The first boys they met weren't chums of theirs. They were the Gaswork Gang!

3. But as the Gasworkers dashed forward to have a fight – Big Joe had a super idea. "Start hitting each other with rubber bricks, Gang!" he hissed. The Gang caught on and began heaving the bricks about! And the Gasworks bullies thought the bricks were real – just as Big Joe had planned!

4. Off went the Gasworkers! They weren't going to stand up to tough boys and girls who didn't even blink when they were hit by bricks. Not likely! "Ho, ho!" laughed Snooty. "Three cheers for us!" But Scrapper had a feeling the Gasworks boys would discover they'd been properly diddled.

5. Snooty had the answer to that. "Build a wall with the rubber bricks, chums!" he said. "Then we'll be ready to repel the invaders if they come back!" So the gang built a rubber wall – and just in time, too. The Gasworkers soon heard how they'd been fooled and back they charged!

6. Snooty and his pals stood with their backs to the wall, grinning like Cheshire cats on a fishing boat. The Gasworkers were big and tough, but Snooty's Gang didn't give that a thought. "Right!" shouted Snooty and his chums dodged cleverly out of the way as the ugly bullies charged.

7. Have you ever hit a rubber wall at full speed? This one gave the Gasworkers a fright. The wall bent back – and back – under the weight of the bullies. Then – PYONNG! – it sprang upright like a ruler firing a pellet – and fired the Gasworkers back the way they had come. That shook them!

Snooty's pals are very sure — their bricks make comfy furniture!

8. "Ow! We've been stabbed!" The bullies howled. They'd landed in a thorn bush; that's why! But Snooty and his chums were very kind to the bullies. They removed the thorns from them at a penny a time! "We'll have no more trouble with them today," said Snooty. He was right!

9. But having had some fun with the bricks, Snooty and his pals began to think of making something useful with them. "What about building rubber furniture?" said Snooty. "A good idea!" agreed the gang. So they all went to work with glue and hand trowels. It was great fun while it lasted.

10. Swanky and Thomas made a bed of bricks and a brick pillow and blanket to match. Snatchy made an easy chair – it was easy to make, too! He slapped rubber bricks together in no time while Snitchy made a rubber foot-rest – for tired feet! Snooty acted as foreman to see there were no slackers!

11. Then, of course, the gang had to try the furniture out. That was a bit of a snag! For, once they tried out the comfy furniture they didn't want to get up. It was too much like work! But when Snooty hit on the idea of selling their comfy furniture – the gang were on their feet in a flash!

12. When all the furniture had been tested, Snooty put up notices on the castle wall to attract buyers. "This ought to bring the tired folk along," he said. It wasn't long before some interested customers flocked into the castle to see the amazing furniture. Big folk, fat folk, short and tall!

13. "All our own work," said Snooty. "Beds, sofas, easy chairs – everything you need in the way of comfy furniture. But don't just take my word for it, try it. Then you'll want to buy it." Snooty was beaming with pride as he led the way – but you know what comes after pride! A fall!

Snooty's bricks are up for sale — as "rubber-outers" they can't fail!

14. Sure enough the fun began. Well, it wasn't exactly fun for Snooty and his pals. The customers didn't sit down gently on the furniture. They jumped up and down on it. In half a tick they were being fired round the room like human cannonballs. Crack! One of them went through the ceiling.

Crunch! Bump! That was another one raising a lump! Whang! Whoof! Another went soaring to the roof. "Ooh!" gulped Snooty, as he started to count up the damage. "We'd have been safer making ordinary furniture like sensible people!" Even Aunt Mat got the fright of her life!

15. But there wasn't any time to cry over spilt milk! The gang had to get busy giving the customers first-aid for their bruises. And the customers didn't even offer to pay for the sticking plaster and bandages. Aunt Mat had to pay – and she told the gang what she thought of them.

16. When the customers had gone Aunt Mat started making out the bill. What with holes in the roof, broken vases – not forgetting the bandages – the total was £20. And Aunt Mat decided to take it off the gang's pocket money. That meant no pocket money till next Christmas! What a thought!

17. That was a black look-out for the gang. "Rubber bricks!" moaned Snooty. "RUBBER BRICKS! I hate 'em!" So the pals fetched knives and hatchets and began to cut the bricks up into pieces. They enjoyed that. They sliced them, chopped them and chipped chunks off them.

18. Snooty had another plan. They weren't just chopping the bricks up in a temper. Oh, no! They were making them into rubbers to sell. And they sold like hot cakes – hot cakes of rubber. And very soon they had enough money to pay Aunt Mat and to buy double helpings of ice-cream, too!

KORKY the Cat AND THE KITS

TO THE BEACH →

YIPPEE! WE'RE GOING TO THE SEASIDE.

YES, AND THE CHANGE WILL DO US GOOD.

THANKS FOR BUYING US A BEACH BALL, UNCLE.

GLOOM! THIS IS DAYLIGHT ROBBERY.

NEVER MIND. THE CHANGE WILL DO YOU GOOD.

GIFTS

CARDS

DRAT! ITS NOZZLE'S COME OUT.

HISS!

BOOT!

AW, NAW!

SNORE!

MAYBE HE CAN HELP

OO-ER! I THINK HE'S OVERDONE IT.

WHEEZE!

WHASSAT?

PRASP!

COME BACK!

HUH?!?

Soon—

WHY'S THIS PLACE SO COLD? MUST SEE THE JANITOR.

BOILER ROOM

IT'S THAT FIRE-EATER'S SON! HE'S GUZZLED ALL THE COAL FOR THE BOILER!

EMPTY

COAL

R-O-A-R!

So—

I'VE HAD ENOUGH OF THIS!

CIRCUS

THESE CHILDREN OF YOURS ARE CAUSING HAVOC!

ONLY ONE WAY TO DEAL WITH THEM!

So—

GREAT LION TAMER I MAKE, EH?

SWISH!

SWISH!

THOSE CROWS AIN'T SCARED OF NUTHIN'!

WELL — NO GOOSEBERRIES, NO PIES!

FLOUR

And so —

THIS'LL SCARE 'EM TO DEATH!

KRAAA!

WHAT IS IT? IS IT A PLANE?

SUPERMAN?

NO! IT'S DESPERATE DAN!

CRASH!

ZONK!

HAPPY LANDINGS, DAN.

Meanwhile —

WHERE IS HE WITH THOSE GOOSE-BERRIES?

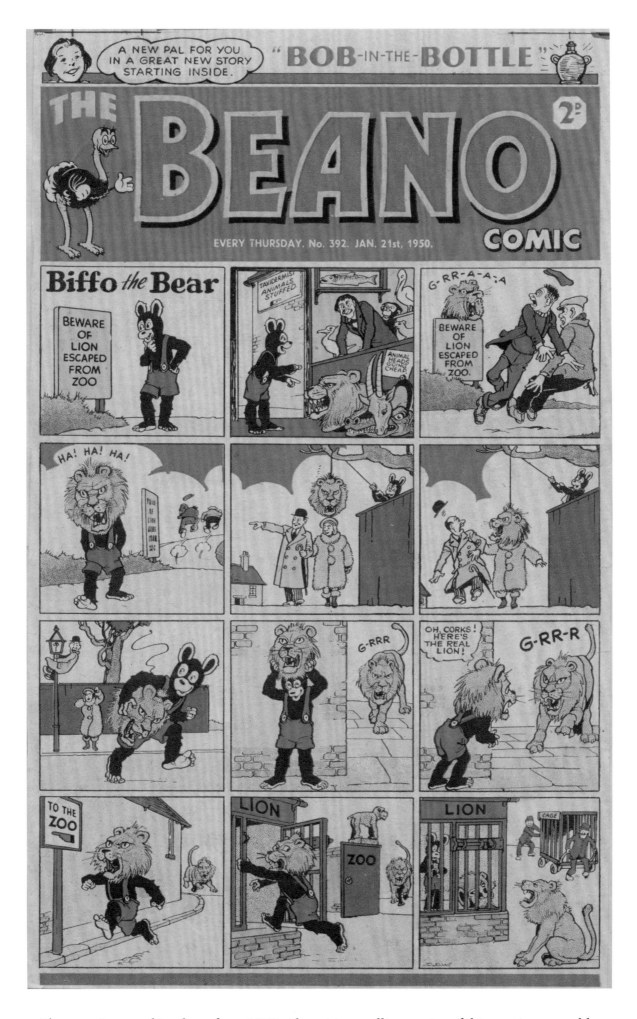

The amazing pranking bear from 1950. Almost two million copies of this comic were sold.

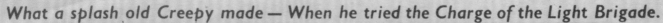

Winker WATSON

YOU THIRD FORM BOYS ARE A DISGRACE — ALWAYS DIRTY AND UNTIDY! I SHALL INSPECT YOU AGAIN AT 4 O'CLOCK AND I WANT TO SEE YOU ALL SPOTLESS!

THE Head was on a tour of inspection at Greytowers School. That was how Winker Watson and his pals came to a get a telling-off . . .

BRR! THE WATER'S C-COLD!

GOLLY, IT'S FREEZING, WINKER!

Winker didn't fancy a cold shower today.

So the wily wangler cleaned himself in a special way!

THANKS FOR THE WARNING, CHAPS. I WON'T BOTHER ABOUT A SHOWER - I'LL JUST POWDER OVER THE DIRTY BITS!

POWDERED CHALK

Mr Creep. the Form Three Housemaster. put up a notice.

NOTICE
ANY BOY FROM FORM III FOUND WITH DIRTY FACE, HANDS OR KNEES WILL BE CANED!
BY ORDER

So did Winker — on the garden gate.

Filled with curiosity, Creepy stalked over.

DANGER! OUT OF BOUNDS TO ALL MASTERS

What cheek! No place was out of bounds to a Housemaster.

But the door wouldn't budge. This called for a shoulder charge.

THE DOOR APPEARS TO BE JAMMED — I'LL HAVE TO USE FORCE . . . . . . CHARGE!

DANGER! OUT OF BOUNDS TO ALL MASTERS

However, the master's shoulder didn't connect.

CALAMITY! IT WAS OPEN ALL THE TIME . . . OO! I CAN'T STOP . . .

HEE-HEE! OPEN SESAME!

Wily Winker had unbolted the door and swung it open with split-second timing.

WHOOPS! RIGHT INTO THE LILY POND!

SPLASH! Creepy's headlong charge ended in a headlong dive.

UGH!

Creepy floundered about in the water. Winker rushed to rescue him from the ankle-deep pond.

DON'T PANIC, SIR — HERE'S A ROPE . . .

Creepy's made to look a clot — By "ham and bacon" on the trot!

The rope was bang on target. It knocked Creepy flying.

THWACK!

UGH! I SUPPOSE THE BOY MEANT WELL....

Creepy surfaced for the second time, a wet and woebegone figure.

OOPS! SORRY, SIR! I'LL RUN AND FETCH YOUR OTHER SUIT!

HURRY, WATSON, I'M SHIVERING!

As Winker returned with Creepy's best suit, a suitable wangle occurred to him.

MMM?

THE SCHOOL PIGGERY

The wangler opened the pig-sty door. Snorting, the porkers charged out straight at Winker.

HELP, SIR, THE PIGS ARE AFTER ME!

OINK! OINK! OINK!

Twenty yards from the pond, Winker faked a fall in the path of the pig stampede.

OOPS! I'VE TRIPPED, SIR — AND THERE GOES YOUR SUIT....

SHOO, YOU BRUTES...

OINK! OINK!

The pigs swept over the suit, then brushed Creepy into the pond.

SORRY, SIR, I'LL HAVE TO GO NOW — IT'S TIME FOR THE HEADMASTER'S INSPECTION!

Alas! Creepy's suit was in a grubby state now!

MY SUIT! DRAT THOSE PIGS!

OINK!

The Head inspected—but he saw no improvement.

YOU THIRD FORM BOYS ARE AN ABSOLUTE DISGRACE! WHAT WOULD MR. CREEP SAY IF HE SAW YOU NOW....

S-SORRY I'M LATE, HEADMASTER, BUT....

MR. CREEP!! HOW DARE YOU...

Gosh! Creepy was ten times dirtier than the dirtiest Third Former —thanks to Winker's dirty tricks!

NOW LISTEN TO ME, CREEP, IT'S UP TO YOU TO SET A GOOD EXAMPLE....

GOOD OLD WINKER! SAVED AGAIN!

The Third Form was dismissed—without punishment! The Head was too busy giving Creepy a dressing-down. Hurrah for Winker! Some wangler!

Next week — A thing to make all schoolboys quake — A special cane that cannot break!

Ivy the Terrible had pranking in her DNA. Bob Nixon, the artist who first drew her, was also the Roger the Dodger artist.

Muddy capers — soggy papers!

Little Plum arrived in The Beano in over sixty years ago. His ability to out-prank the crazy wildlife that shared his world ensured his survival.

Plum was much smaller but much smarter than the Big Chiefy of the tribe.

Lessons in pranking from The Beano's geriatric delinquent Grandpa. Amazingly Grandpa was still kept in line by his father – how old was he? Is pranking the secret to long life?

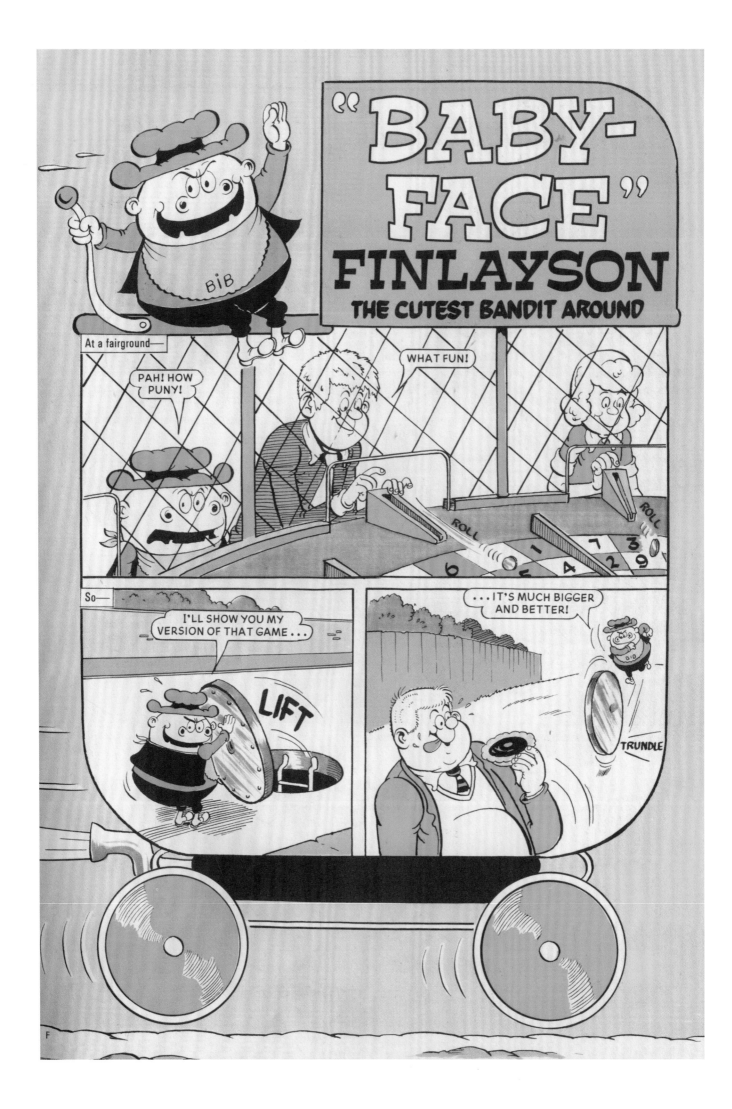

Plane crash—big splash!

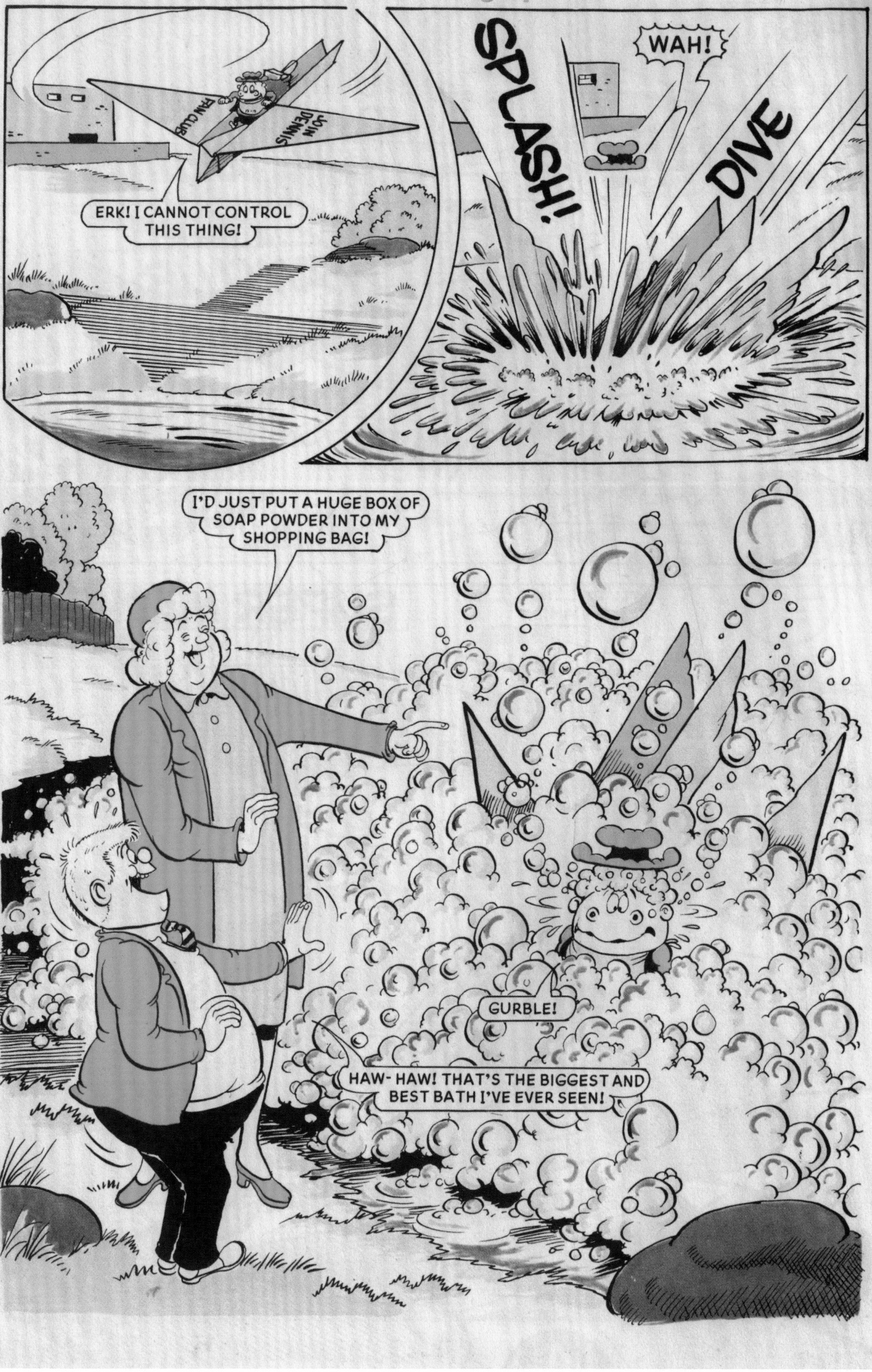

ROGER the DODGER

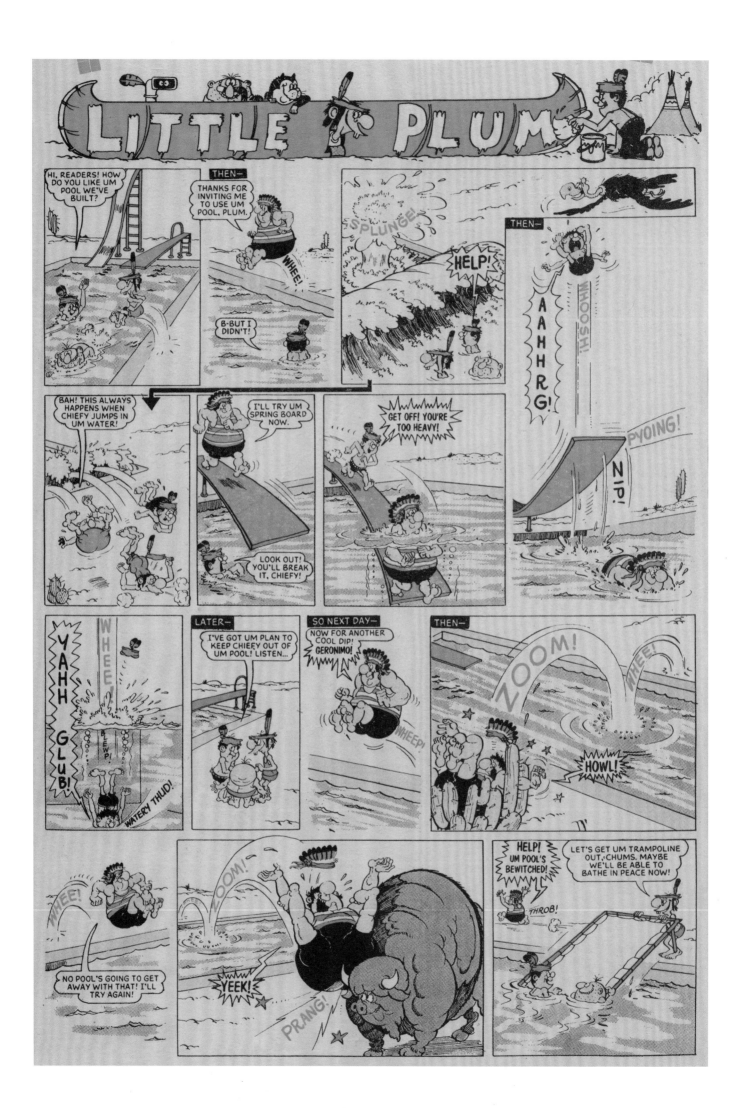

MINNIE the MINX

THE BEANO 2D

EVERY THURSDAY   No. 585. OCT. 3rd, 1953.

Biffo the BEAR

NOW FOR A BIG BREAKFAST!

POOR BUSTER! HE DOES LOOK HUNGRY!

GOSH, I'M SORRY, BUSTER! I'D SHARE MY BREAKFAST WITH YOU, BUT THERE'S REALLY ONLY ENOUGH FOR ONE! HONEST!

IT'S A DUMMY! AND WHILE I WAS SPEAKING TO IT THE REAL BUSTER TOOK MY BREAKFAST!

LATER

LORD MAYOR'S TREAT — ON NOW —

COME IN! EVERYONE'S WELCOME!

A DUMMY CAN'T EAT, BUT I CAN EAT HIS SHARE!

FOR BIFFO   FOR BUSTER

DON'T BE GREEDY, BUSTER, YOU CAN'T HAVE A SECOND TREAT!

LORD MAYOR'S TREAT — ON NOW —

HA! HA! I TRICKED YOU WITH YOUR OWN DUMMY!

THE BEANO

EVERY THURSDAY   No. 578. AUG. 15th, 1953.   2ᴰ

THE DANDY COMIC

Nº 122 · MAR. 30TH 1940
EVERY FRIDAY
2D

KORKY THE CAT

KORKY'S FIRST OF APRIL JAPE
JUST MAKES HIM LOSE HIS WOOL.
FOR KORKY'S KICKS ALL GO ASTRAY —
NOW HE'S THE APRIL FOOL !

THE BASH STREET KIDS

THERE'S SOMETHING AFOOT!

PSSST! I WANT A ONE-WAY TICKET TO AUSTRALIA!

TRAVEL AGENCY — GET YOUR TRAVEL TICKETS HERE

I KNOW WHAT'S GOING ON. TEACHER'S EMIGRATING TO AUSTRALIA!

THIS BASH ST. SPIES ARE STILL WATCHING

I'M LEAVING NOW. I'M FINISHED WITH THOSE AWFUL BASH ST. KIDS FOR EVER!

I'LL LEAVE BY THE WINDOW. NOBODY WILL KNOW I'VE GONE!

FUNNY TIME OF NIGHT TO HAVE A BATH, TEACHER!

TWO HOURS LATER — TEACHER TRIES AGAIN

NOBODY WILL KNOW ME IN THIS DISGUISE!

THAT'S A FUNNY-LOOKING SWEEP WITH A MORTAR-BOARD... IT'S TEACHER!

WE WON'T LET HIM GET AWAY, CHAPS!

GRAB HIM, FELLAS!

YOU WON'T STOP ME! NOTHING WILL STOP ME. I'M GOING ON BOARD NOW!

YOU CAN'T GO ON BOARD SHIP SMELLING LIKE THAT, TEACHER. HAVE SOME SCENT!

THAT SCENT SPRAY WAS REALLY A PAINT SPRAY. IT WORKED!

GET ASHORE, MISTER! YOU'VE GOT SPOTS ALL OVER YOU. WE CAN'T TAKE YOU ON THIS SHIP. YOU'VE GOT MEASLES OR SOMETHING!

BUT TEACHER HASN'T GIVEN UP TRYING

SNIGGER

TEACHER MYSTERIOUSLY DISAPPEARED. I BET HE'S INSIDE THAT CRATE BEING LOADED ON TO THE SHIP!

TICKLE THE MAN AT THE WINCH, CHAPS!

HE! HE! HE-HE! HE!

WHAT'S GONE WRONG NOW?

HELP! THE SHIP'S SAILING — AND WE'RE STILL ON BOARD!

WE'RE OFF TO AUSTRALIA INSTEAD OF TEACHER!

HELLO! I WANT TO MAKE A 'PHONE CALL TO AUSTRALIA! HURRY! HURRY!

THE RESULT OF THAT PHONE CALL MEANS A BUSY TIME FOR THE POSTMEN DOWN UNDER!

THANK GOODNESS! WE WERE TOLD THEY WERE COMING!

WE GOT OUT IN THE NICK OF TIME!

WE'LL BE SAFER IN BRITAIN!

GOSH! THERE ARE HUNDREDS OF SHIPS ALL SAILING THE OTHER WAY! AND THEY'RE LOADED WITH PEOPLE. WONDER WHY?

MEANWHILE THE BASH ST. KIDS ARE WELL ON THE WAY TO AUSTRALIA

THE KIDS ARE IN AUSTRALIA NOW

NOW WE KNOW WHY ALL THESE SHIPS WERE SAILING THE OTHER WAY! THE POPULATION OF AUSTRALIA'S EMIGRATED TO BRITAIN!

It is very fitting that we end this prank-fest with Dennis the Menace. He has consistently been the most prolific and imaginative of pranksters – and remember, he was playing in a very tough league.

Great rivals such as Roger the Dodger, Winker Watson, Minnie the Minx and even the madcap bear, Biffo, all came close. But Dennis beats them all and we give him the title of – PRANK MASTER!

Published by DC Thomson Annuals Ltd in 2015. DC Thomson Annuals Ltd, 185 Fleet Street, London EC4A 2HS